German Minefields at Alamein: October-November 1942

War Dept. Office of the Chief of Engineers

The BiblioGov Project is an effort to expand awareness of the public documents and records of the U.S. Government via print publications. In broadening the public understanding of government and its work, an enlightened democracy can grow and prosper. Ranging from historic Congressional Bills to the most recent Budget of the United States Government, the BiblioGov Project spans a wealth of government information. These works are now made available through an environmentally friendly, print-on-demand basis, using only what is necessary to meet the required demands of an interested public. We invite you to learn of the records of the U.S. Government, heightening the knowledge and debate that can lead from such publications.

Included are the following Collections:

Budget of The United States Government
Presidential Documents
United States Code
Education Reports from ERIC
GAO Reports
History of Bills
House Rules and Manual
Public and Private Laws

Code of Federal Regulations
Congressional Documents
Economic Indicators
Federal Register
Government Manuals
House Journal
Privacy act Issuances
Statutes at Large

WAR DEPARTMENT, CHIEF OF ENGINEERS
    German minefields at Alamein, October-
  November 1942.

M 9405
G10
H1
c.42

——PROPERTY OF U. S. ARMY

WAR DEPARTMENT
Office of The Chief of Engineers
Washington, D. C.

28 June 1943.

Information Bulletin No. 124.

Subject: German Minefields at Alamein.
(October - November, 1942).

    The accompanying report from British sources on enemy minefields at Alamein is published for the information of all concerned. This is the most complete and succinct report published to date.

    A glossary of words and abbreviations has been added at the end of the report.

                              C. L. Sturdevant,
                               Brigadier General,
                        Assistant Chief of Engineers.

ARMY MAP SERVICE, U. S. ARMY, WASHINGTON, D. C., 200515
1943

Information Bulletin)   WAR DEPARTMENT
                        Office of the Chief of Engineers
No. 124   )   29 June 1943.

GERMAN MINEFIELDS AT ALAMEIN

LAYOUT OF ENEMY MINEFIELDS

1. DEFINITIONS
   (a) Mine Belt is that portion of a Minefield which contains mines
       laid to a regular pattern and of the ordered number of mines
       per yard of front.

   (b) Mine Field is the area which contains one or more of the belts
       referred to above, but at the same time, containing several
       areas in addition, of scattered mines.

   Below in Figure 1 is shown a Typical Enemy Protective Minefield,
   with dimensions:-

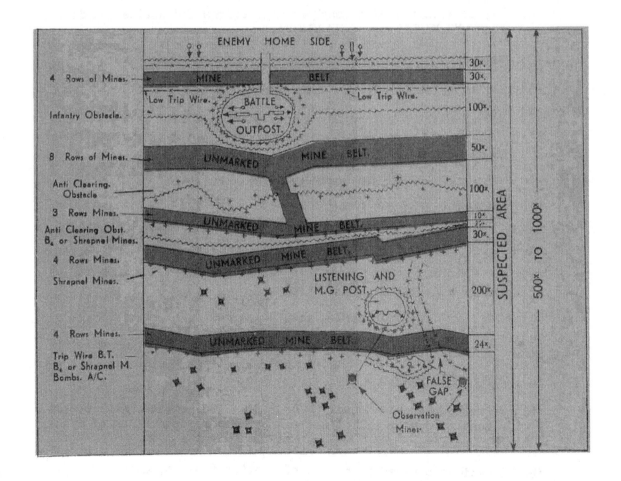

Figure 1. Typical Enemy Protective Minefield.

2. **MINEFIELDS**

   (1) **MARKING**

(A)   Protective Minefields:

   (1) The forward edge is often unmarked. When it is marked, it will be with false gaps, leading onto mines; with tactical wiring not beneficial to the attacker, wire obstacles to neutralize mechanical clearing devices and most types of anti-personnel device and automatic sentry. Unmarked mines are likely to be scattered about also.

   (2) The rear edge is normally marked, low and high wire, Dannert Coils, cairns etc., all being used for this purpose.

(B)   TACTICAL MINEFIELDS

   (1) In many cases no marking at all.

   (2) May be well fenced or marked small cairns and notice boards "ACHTUNG MINEN" or "ZONE MINATA."

   (3) Marked by track along front.

   (4) Marked by plough furrow along front.

   (5) Marked with cairns on 40 gal drums at corners.

(C)   DUMMY FIELDS Main Axis only.
                Naturally well marked. Notice Boards etc.
                May be Booby-Trapped.

(D)   DELAYED FIELDS
                Generally very obscure. Often laid in vicinity of some very recognisable feature, telegraph pole, kilostone, etc.

(E)   ROADS, DEFILES, BUILT-UP AREAS

                Scattered Mines. Unmarked.

3. GAPS. The following have been reported:

   (a) Width: 10 yds to 7 yds.

   (b1) Normally closed: Usually 2 or 3 rows Tellermines, with boards placed on one or all of the rows to ensure detonation of mines. (Figure 2).

   (b2) Sometimes covered by groups of scattered mines, unmarked, up 2000 yards in front. See Figure 2.

(c) Marking: (a) Painted Signs as in Figure 2.
(b) Patrol Gaps marked by liminous tubes 1" long placed on top of mines and visible for 3 yards.

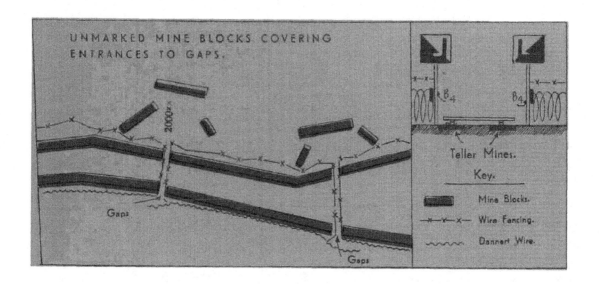

Figure 2. Gaps.

4. MINE BELTS These are usually 2 to 4 rows of mines deep, laid to a simple pattern by pacing, and at about 1 mine per 2 yard front. 2 mines per yard front is only found in road blocks, gaps etc.

   (1) PATTERN

   (a) Regular: This is most common. Mines in rows are spaced at equal distances, with equal distances between rows, the mines of one row being equally spaced between mines of the next.

   The method may be varied by different distances between rows. (Figure 3).

   (2) SPACING: The average observed spacing between mines in a row is 6 yards; never less than 3 yards and seldom greater than 10 yards.

   5 yards and 10 yards are the most common distances. (Figure 3).

   NB: Minimum distance for Tellermines:
       5 paces: cover 8 to 10 cm. (0.32" - .39")
       10 paces cover   5 cm. (0.2"   )

By Night some irregularity is bound to occur.

(3) MINE-LAYING DRILLS

All mine-laying is carried out by pacing drills. Belts are laid in blocks usually on a section basis. The examples in Figure 3 are typical (Average time 5 minutes camouflaged.)

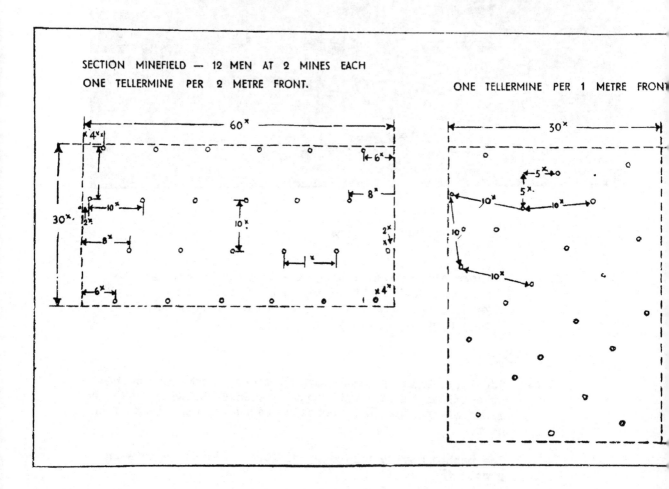

Figure 3. Minefield patterns.

5. TYPES OF MINES
Tellermines, French Mines, CVP, LP 211, Wooden - Improvised Mines (D235 Igniter) British GS 2EP Types. (See WD Training Circular No. 62, 1943.)

6. **METHODS OF LAYING MINES IN FIELDS**

    Unless in very hasty minelaying, mines are dug-in and camouflaged; they are therefore not easy to detect by eye, especially if there have been rain or wind storms. Scrub is used for extra concealment.

(A)   (1) Tellermines and sometimes own mines laid two or three on top of another (Make Tank into Transporter casualty) and booby-trapped.

    (2) Tellermines connected by Cordtex to 2 or more EP Mines close by and also to trip wire picketed out.

    (3) 20% Tellermines booby-trapped. (Handles and Pegs or to each other.)

    (4) French Mines Booby-trapped under lid.

    (5) Stick Grenade tied to base of French mine and pegged down.

    (6) Real Mines interspersed with dummies.

    (7) Metal objects scattered about in field to confuse mine detectors.

    (8) French Mines connected trip wires to S Mines.

(B) **Methods of laying Mines in Roads, Defiles, Tracks & Built-up Areas**

    (1) Mines laid 3 ft deep in tracks likely to rut.

    (2) Augered into hard well used tracks.

    (3) Potholes in Tarmac Roads, Sanded or Tarred over.

    (4) Augered into Road Berms.

    (5) Potholes in concrete, Courtyards etc., cemented over.

    (6) Tellermines connected by pressure bar.

    (7) Tellermines with pull or trip wires as Booby-Traps inside buildings.

7. **BOOBY-TRAPPING.**

    (1) **Minefields.**

        1. **Front Edge.**

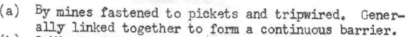

- (a) By mines fastened to pickets and tripwired. Generally linked together to form a continuous barrier.
- (b) S Mines either set out as above with overlapping trip wires or using SMi. Z. 35 Antenna Igniter.
- (c) Aerial Bombs with pull switches generally concealed and connected to trip wires, or to French Mines by FID. (May be in Depth.)
- (d) Wire obstacles, concertina wires tec. connected to charger by pull switches and wires.
- (e) Mortar Bombs buried and activated SMi Z35 in nosecap.
- (f) All notices, Pickets suspect, may be connected to made up charge etc. Skull & Cross Bones notice usually means traps in vicinity.

2. <u>Defensive positions within and behind Minefields.</u>

- (a) Delay action charges in dumps, dugouts, etc.
- (b) Booby-trapped loot.
- (c) Shaving Stick, Bombs, explosive cameras, etc.
- (d) Moveable objects, vehicles, aircraft, etc.
- (e) Usual Trip-wire actuated bombs.

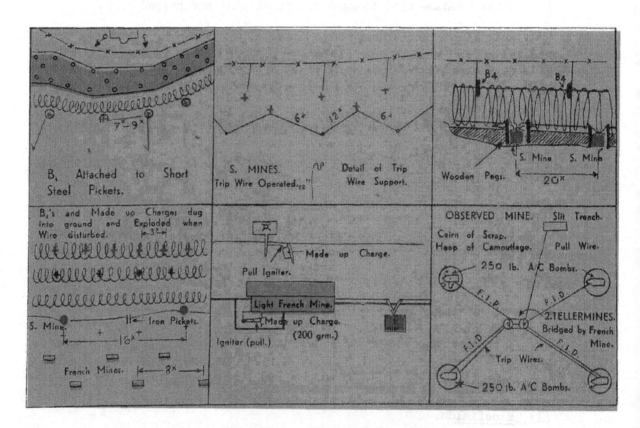

Figure 4. Anti-personnel and activated mines.

(2) **In Built-up Areas.**

Open spaces, courtyards, etc., which might be used for parking M.T. are likely to be well covered with cunningly concealed mines, particularly where vehicles are likely to run off Main Road.

- (1) Tellermines connected to door handles and trip wires across thresholds.
- (2) Stick Grenades etc. tied to door jambs.
- (3) Manhole covers with devices.
- (4) Water points and Services apparatus likely to be Booby-trapped.

ENEMY MINEFIELDS IN THE WESTERN DESERT

Embodying information up to and including the Alamein Line.

1. TYPES OF MINEFIELD

LARGE PROTECTIVE MINEFIELDS

These minefields protect the entire front of a Defensive Position. As the Defence develops in Depth they are further extended in successive lines, and in general follow the growth detailed in the following example.

(a) Example based on the Enemy Defences on the Alamein Line.
(Period of construction 4 months.)

Phase One:
Single continuous line of minefield covering the whole front. (About 200^x between wires.)
This is generally marked on both sides with wire as incomplete parts of the line may have to be held with the help of armour, until they can be filled in with mines.
When this is completed thickening begins, immediately, in front of the forward line of wire.
The whole is covered with close SA and ATk fire, and listening and MG posts interspersed in the minefield.
Behind this barrier the main strong points of the system are being established at 3 to 5 km centres, in mutual support, while the armour moves to the rear for a counter attack role.

Phase Two:
(a) Further thickening of unmarked belt in front of original forward wire. This is complicated by unmarked tactical spurs and small scattered minefields further out. Full use is also made of scattered wire obstacles and false gaps for the unwary. All forms of Anti-personnel devices and numerous automatic sentries are also likely to

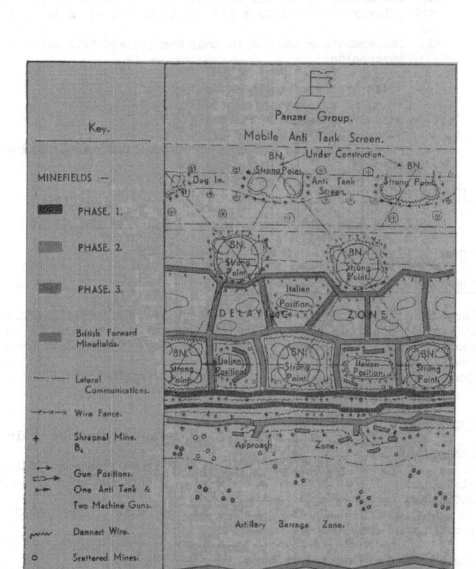

Figure 5. Enemy Defenses on the Alamein Line.

be found in this zone. (Zone may extend 800^x beyond original front wire.)

(b) A second line of minefields, not always conspicuously marked with scattered wire, stone cairns, boxes etc., is formed to protect new main strong points echeloned back from those of the front line, and forming with them, triangles of 3 to 5 km sides (1.9 to 3.1 miles). (These fields 100^x to 200^x deep.)

(c) In order to disorganize and canalize penetration at this stage, the first and second lines are interconnected, and again marked in an apparently haphazard manner to the ground observer. This serves to compartment every success and maintains the element of surprise. (These fields 100^x to 200^x deep.)

NB: The marking of these fields, while not always obvious to the ground observer, is generally very distinct on air photographs.

Phase Three:

A third line of minefields, generally well marked with fences or stone cairns, protects the front and flanks of the Second Line Main Strong points and the front of the Artillery Area. (5 to 6 km (3.1 to 3.7 miles) from front of Minefields.)

NB: TACTICAL SITING OF MINEFIELD:
Enemy Side of Crests (Hull down positions for attacker) extending over skyline where possible.

Troops holding MAIN STRONG POINTS in the front are likely at this stage to be gradually thinned out and a third line of Strong Points put under construction.

During this process further fields and scattered mines (unmarked) may be laid in the Compartments between the Main, First and Second Strong Points. Anti-personnel devices and booby-traps may also be put down.

(The Third Field usually 200^x deep.)

In rear areas tactical and protective Minefields are also likely to be under construction - these will be visible to Air Photo Recce.

In conclusion, it is important to appreciate the process of evolution, as attacks may have to be carried out, supplemented with mine-clearing, at any stage. There is also value in being able to forecast future developments.

(b) Example in Figure 6 is based on Captured Document 19 July 42 (Italian.) (Thought to be a copy of British Methods.)

2. SMALL PROTECTIVE MINEFIELDS:

These may protect Strong Points, either isolated or within a system. They may or may not be obviously marked to the ground observer, but clues are usually visible in air photographs.

3. LARGE TACTICAL FIELDS:

These are designed to restrict the movement of, and also surprise, our patrols and attacking armour in the rear of Strong Point Areas and Defence Lines, where these are capable of being outflanked. These fields are seldom deep, sometimes two or three rows of mines only, and at most 100^X across. They may however be of considerable length. Usually they are marked to escape observation. They are often laid along the line of tracks normal to a likely approach, e.g. Mechill Timimi Area.

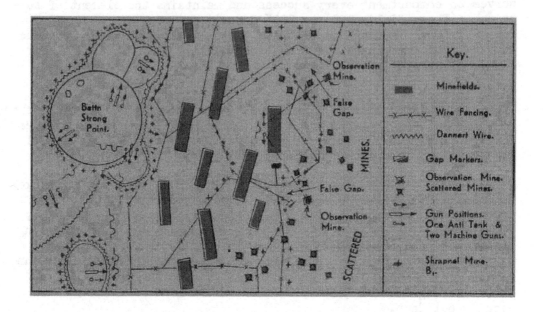

Figure 6. Minefield.

NOTE:
1. False Gaps, and Scattered Minefields and mines unmarked in front.
2. Belts separate but covering each other so there is clear run through.
3. Deceptive Wiring.
4. Perimeter Wire no indication whatever of Mine Belt. The whole depth would have to be swept.

4. SMALL TACTICAL FIELDS:

These are generally used in conjunction with the Large. The main role is usually against Armoured Car Patrols, Recce Columns etc. Defiles and observation areas, track and concealment wadis, patrol lines when known etc., are harassed by small, usually unmarked, scattered minefields. If marked, probably by small cairns at each end only. Where the site is an obvious one, mines will also be laid to catch those avoiding it, e.g. slopes of defiles etc.

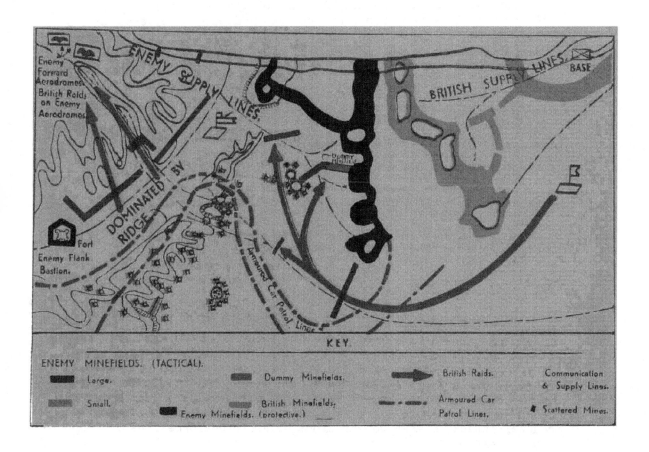

Figure 7. Large Tactical Field.

5. DUMMY FIELDS:

Used in Tactical Role and well marked.

6. SMALL DELAYING FIELDS:

These are likely to be laid during a retreat on roads and tracks vital to the rapid follow-up of the enemy. They are generally unmarked scattered fields with a proportion of Anti-personnel devices, some laid near some recognisable object, e.g. a Kilostone. They are often sited at points where the pursuers may have their attention diverted by fire of rear guards etc. Crest of Rise, Corner etc.

7. CONCLUSION.

The above are the principal types of fields used and it will be clearly seen that the enemy, who has now had much experience in the use of mines, is capable of, and will use, many artifices to increase the effectiveness of his minefields. The importance of exhaustive ground and air recce cannot be over-emphasised before embarking on an attack.

MINING OF ROADS AND BUILT-UP AREAS.

NB:
1. Carried out to impose maximum delay to the Advance where movement is restricted to Road Defiles.
2. Liberal use of Booby-Traps and Anti-personnel Mines.
3. Extensive Mining of Demolitions and Deviations.
4. Deliberate Mining in Berms, Passing Places and at Road Junctions, made difficult to detect, designed against volume of transport (echelons etc.) supporting advance.
5. 20% of Mines in road Booby-trapped.
6. Built-up Areas, Deliberate Mining and Booby-Trapping.

THE PASSAGE OF ENEMY DEFENCES IN DEPTH

GENERAL: The steady development of Enemy defensive technique, integrated large scale minefields, the immediate close covering fire of which is linked into the fire plan; coupled with organisation in depth, observed artillery fire, armoured counter attack against points of penetration, has greatly increased the formidability of such systems to mechanised forces. Heavy air attack may also be encountered. The object of the defence is to wear down an attack, prior to powerful counter attack against penetrations by armoured formations held in mobile reserve.

German Theory intends, by organisation in depth, a series of mutually supporting Strong Points, of all round defence, echeloned back. Minefields to be used as the complement of the maximum fire power of the defensive fire plan, frontal protection, all round protection of Strong Points; delaying zones, protection of field artillery zones, and lateral communications.

Penetration will be canalised and destroyed, while surprise will be maintained in depth.

The enemy has now had considerable experience and much subterfuge may be employed to further his ends.

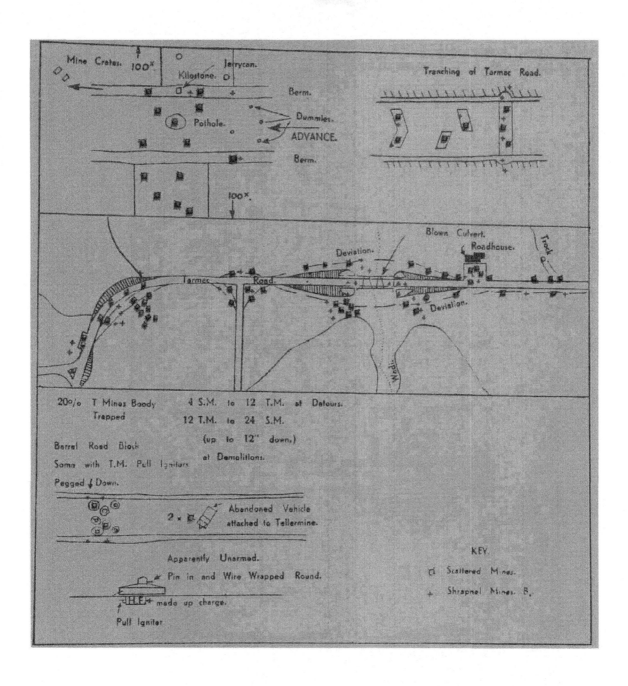

Figure 8. Mining of Roads.

The diagram above is based on German Theory and is verified by the defences found on the ground. In practice asymmetry will be dictated, to some extent, by the ground formation.

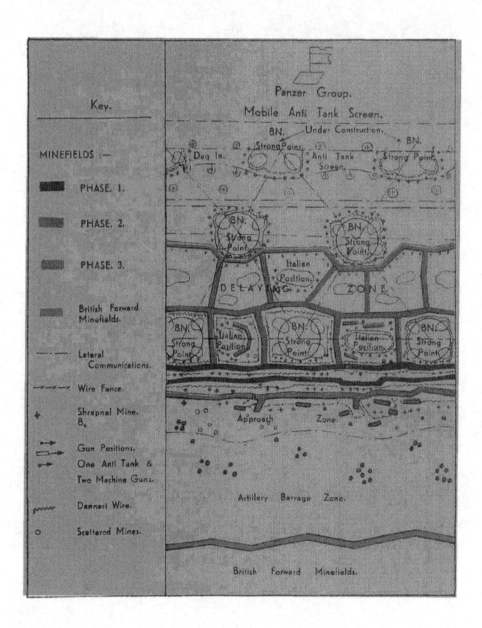

Figure 9. Enemy Defenses on the Alamein Line.

The power of a defence of the above type is such, that the operation of overrunning static positions, and forcing a passage for support weapons to hold off counter attack, armour to engage the enemy mobile groups, and/or effect a break through, assumes major dimensions. The following are some of the principal factors:-

(1) Intensive preparatory reconnaissance, using all ground and air photographic resources, to ascertain the extent, depth and stage of development of the defences. Indication of the points and weight of attack necessary will be gained.

(2) An assault crossing by foot infantry to establish Bridgeheads under the cover of which passages may be cleared for support weapons and armour.

(3) Intense artillery support.

(4) Local Air Superiority. Air protection for the communications defile formed by a passage is imperative.

(5) The cover of darkness (Moonlight).

(6) Complete surprise as to intended Bridgeheads and Armoured Breakthrough
Involving:-
    (a) Elaborate long term plans for deception during assembly and approach.
    (b) Long approach marches (by night) from assembly areas, sufficiently in rear to conceal the intention, and in the case of armour, through the overrun defences into the open enemy rear (by first light.)
    Problems of organization, preparation of approach routes, traffic control and regulation are extremely complicated.

(7) Specialised equipment for the detection, clearing, marking and control of the gaps through minefields.

(8) A.A. protection of the defile.

The extent of the problems thereby produced, infers an appreciable period of preparation, and requires intimate co-operation between all arms, with a high standard of staff work for the execution of plans based upon them.
    Forcing and maintenance of the passage will be merged by the constant threat to a communications defile in close proximity to the enemy.

BRIDGEHEAD:
    The preliminary establishment of a BRIDGEHEAD after an assault crossing by infantry equipped with Bangalore torpedoes, grapnels, etc.,

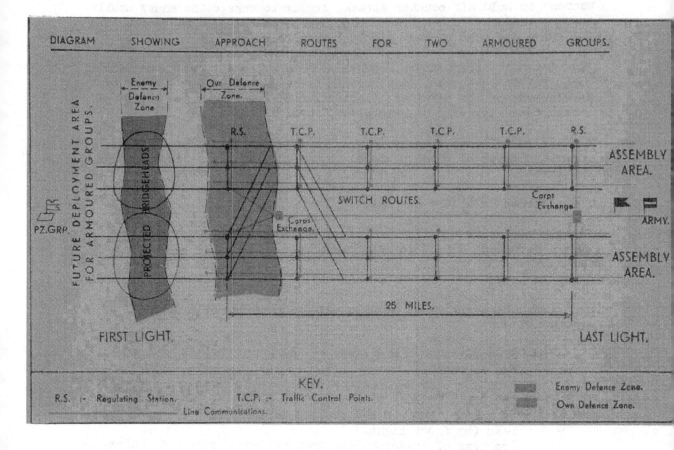

Figure 10. Approach and switch routes and permanent
telephone communications for control points.

for dealing with A.Personnel and Booby Trap obstacles, is a vital
factor. Only under its protective cover can the actual clearance of
a passage be effected by the R.E. (who can either fight or work but
not both at the same time.)
An operation of this scale by night or by day is not expected to
achieve 100% mopping up. The clearance parties should therefore
possess attached fire power to deal with overrun pockets of resistance

opposing their immediate operations.
The Minefield Task Force is a solution to this problem and a suggested composition for an Armd. Div. requiring three routes is:-

Task Force H.Q.

Bn. Motor Bde less Coys A.B.C. & 3 Tps Mortar Coy.
C.R.E. Armd. Div.
Sigs. Det.
R.A.P.
Sqn. R.E. (C.R.E's. Reserve.)

ROUTE 1 Route Force	ROUTE 2 Route Force	ROUTE 3 Route Force
A Coy Bn Motor Bde	B Coy Bn Motor Bde	C Coy Bn Motor Bde
1 Tp Mortar Coy above	2 Tp Mortar Coy above	3 Tp Mortar Coy above
Sqn R.E.	Sqn R.E.	Sqn R.E.
Det Pro.	Det Pro.	Det Pro.
Tp Armd Regt.	Tp Armd Regt.	Tp Armd Regt.
L.O. HQ Armd Bde.	L.O. HQ Armd Bde.	L.O. HQ Armd Bde
R.A.P.	R.A.P.	R.A.P.
Det Route Marking.	Det Route Marking.	Det Route Marking.

CLEARANCE & ROUTE MARKING:

Standardisation of the drill for Detection, clearance and marking of Routes (and the necessary equipment) by R.E. and the practice of all arms in marching to the marking signs by day and night, throughout the entire force taking part in the attack, will greatly enhance flexibility of command allowing interchanges of sectors and axes of passage during battle.

COMMUNICATIONS:

The importance of reliable, adequate and secure communications cannot be over-emphasised. Ground line will be necessary as far as possible for security. Duplication by R/T for emergency and use of forward elements unknowns:-

1. Gaining of Objectives, and the time by Inf. Div carrying out the assault crossing.

2. Which of the projected gaps can be commenced and completed and therefore which routes can be realised as passages.

3. Times of completion and opening for traffic of the gaps.

Figure 11 shows the Order of March of an Armoured Div. following up a BRIDGEHEAD assault by an Inf. Div. Communications Should be Noted.

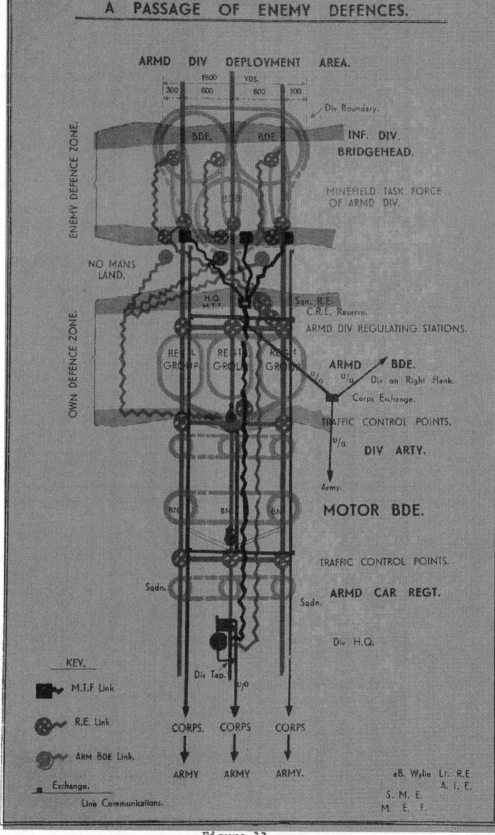

Figure 11.

GLOSSARY

Achtung Minen (German)	—	Attention! Mines
Bde	—	Brigade
Cordtex	—	Similar to primacord.
Coys	—	Companies
C.R.E.	—	Commander, Royal Engineers
Dannert Coils	—	Similar to Concertina Wire
Det Pro	—	Detachment provost (M.P.)
FID	—	Fuse ignition device
L.O.	—	Liaison officer
R.A.P.	—	Regiment aid post
R.E.	—	Royal Engineers
Recce	—	Reconnaissance
R/T	—	Radio telephony
Tps	—	Troops
x (as 2000^x)	—	Yards
Zona Minata (Italian)	—	Mine Zone.

CPSIA information can be obtained
at www.ICGtesting.com
Printed in the USA
LVOW03s1828281115

464508LV00017B/539/P